BROADWAY'S BEST

ISBN 978-1-4803-4431-0

HAL•LEONARD®
CORPORATION
7777 W. BLUEMOUND RD. P.O. BOX 13819 MILWAUKEE, WI 53213

Visit Hal Leonard Online at
www.halleonard.com

ABOUT A QUARTER TO NINE

from 42nd STREET

Lyrics by AL DUBIN
Music by HARRY WARREN

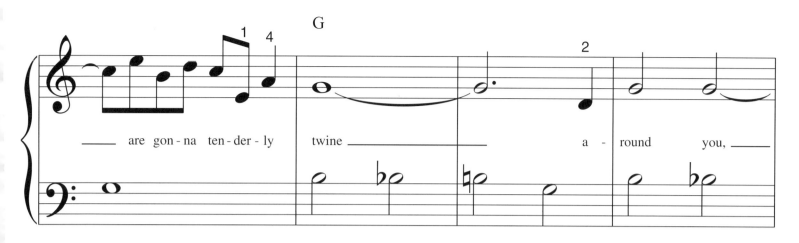

are gon - na ten - der - ly twine _____ a - round you, _____

_____ a - round a quar - ter to nine. I know I

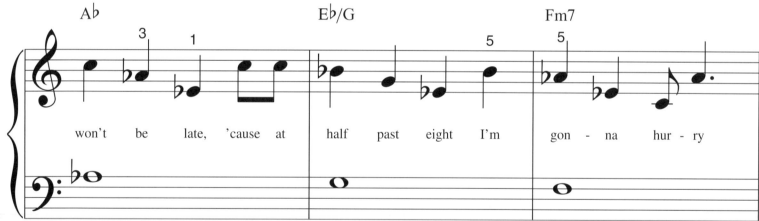

won't be late, 'cause at half past eight I'm gon - na hur - ry

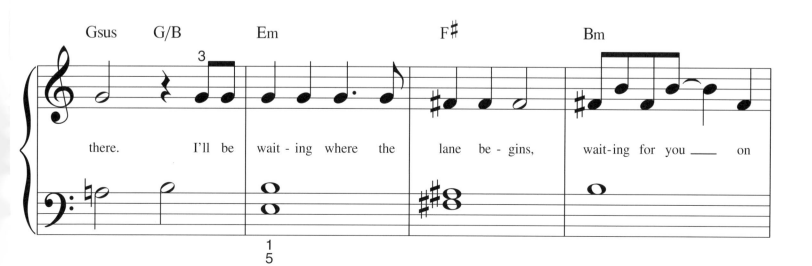

there. I'll be wait - ing where the lane be - gins, wait-ing for you _____ on

BUT NOT FOR ME

from GIRL CRAZY

Music and Lyrics by GEORGE GERSHWIN
and IRA GERSHWIN

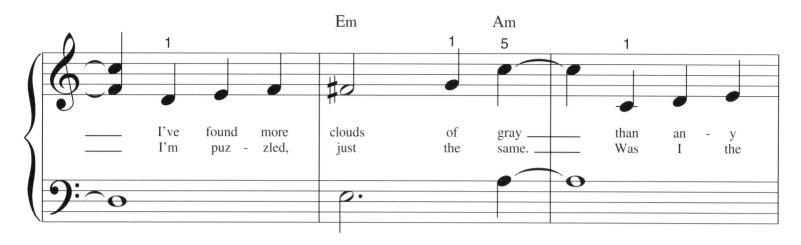

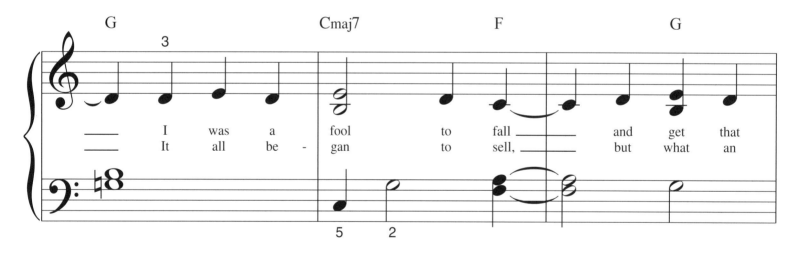

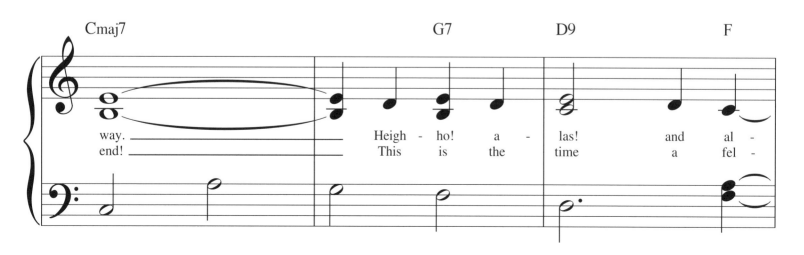

AQUARIUS

from the Broadway Musical Production HAIR

Words by JAMES RADO and GEROME RAGNI
Music by GALT MacDERMOT

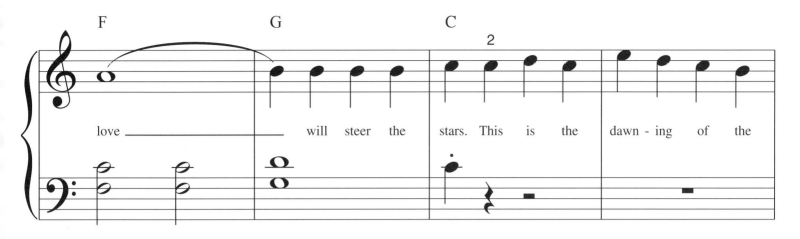

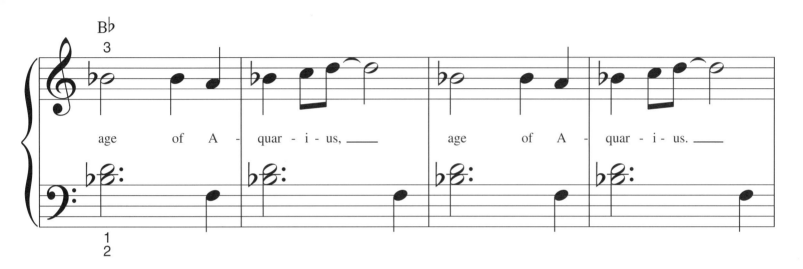

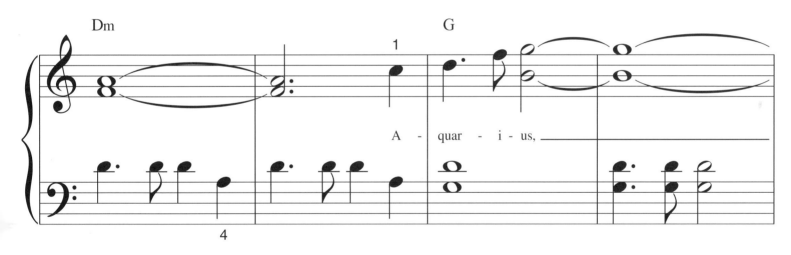

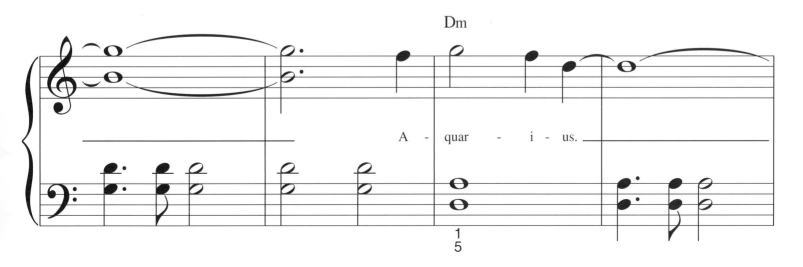

DEFYING GRAVITY
from the Broadway Musical WICKED

Music and Lyrics by
STEPHEN SCHWARTZ

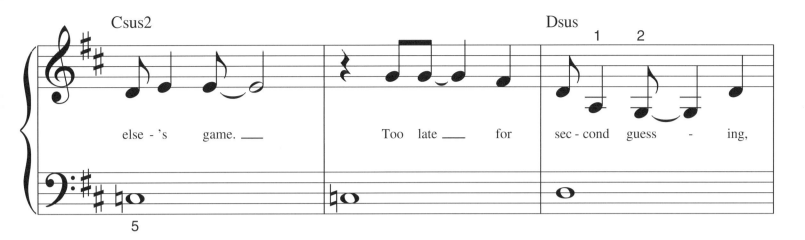

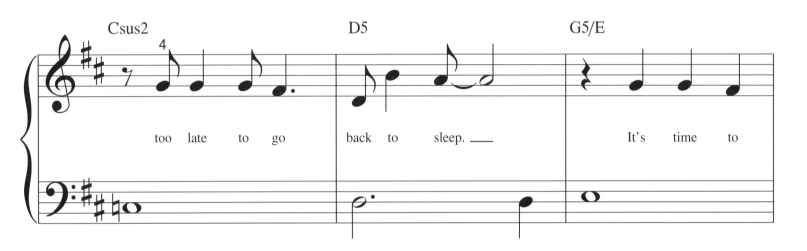

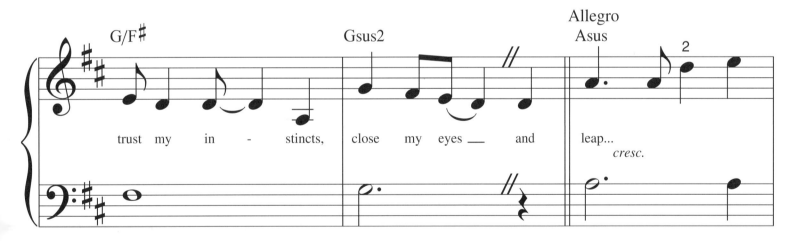

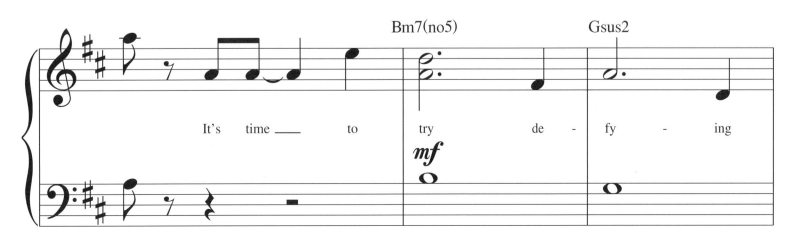

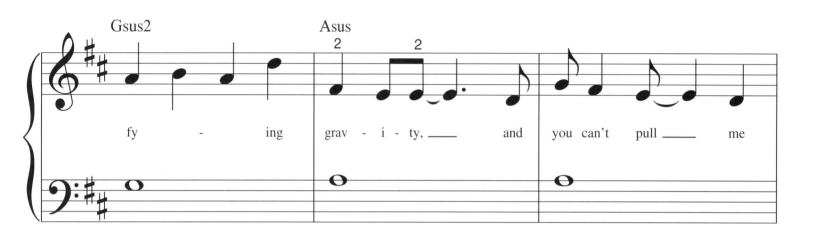

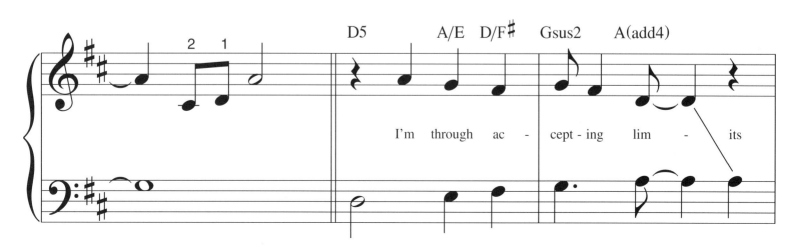

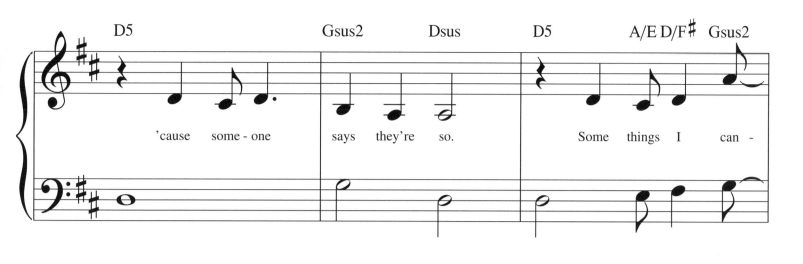

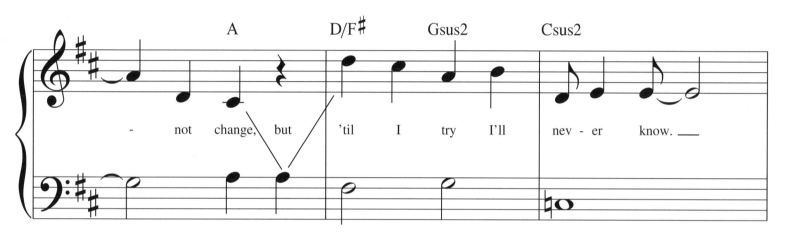

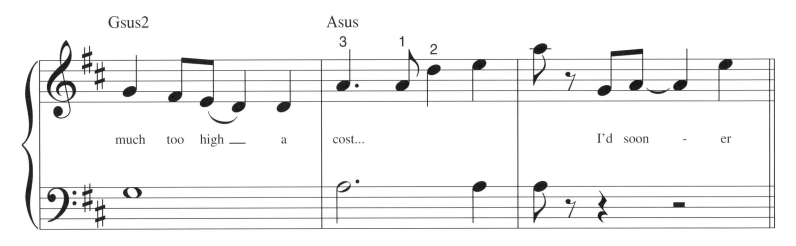

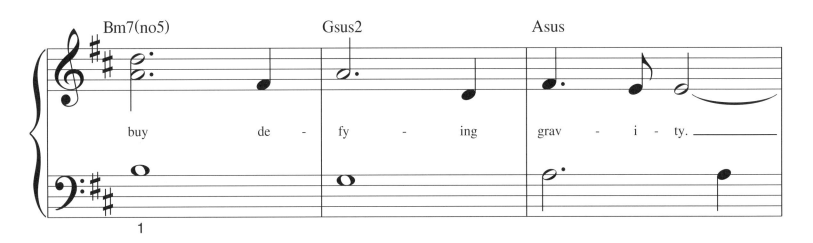

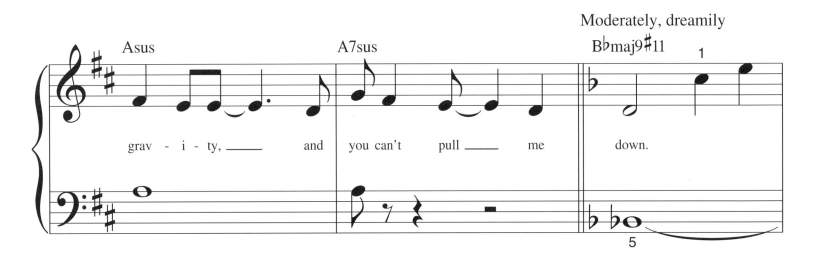

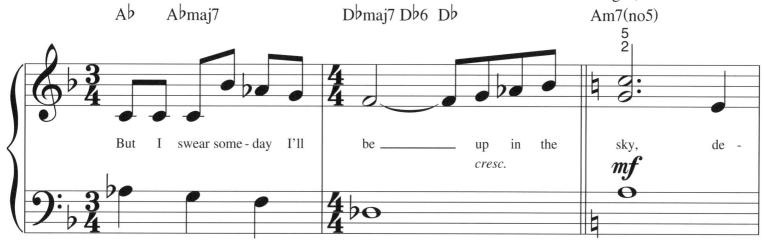

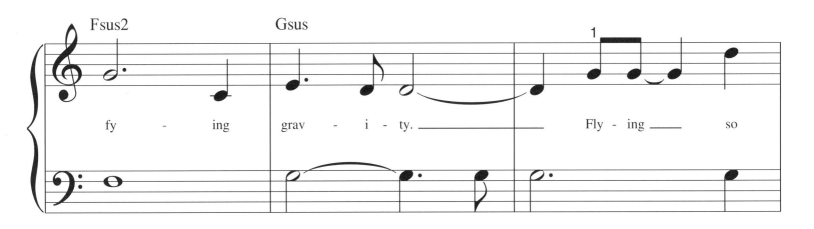

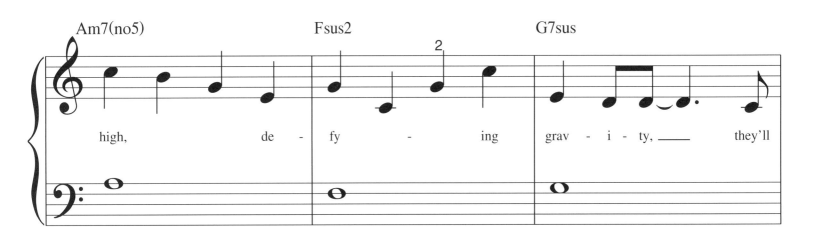

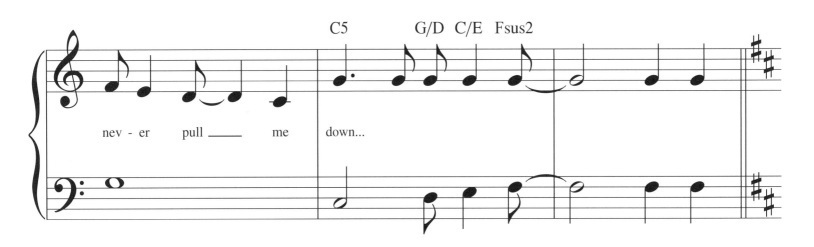

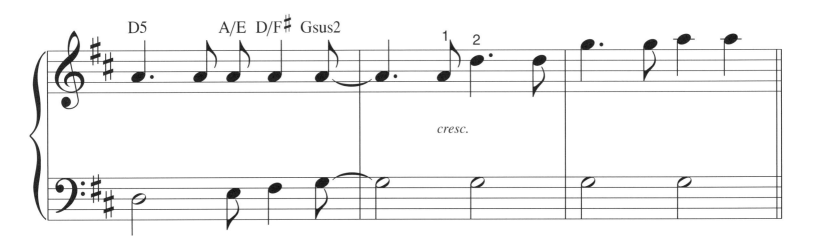

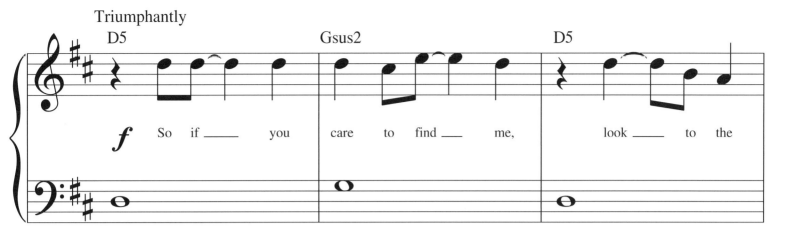

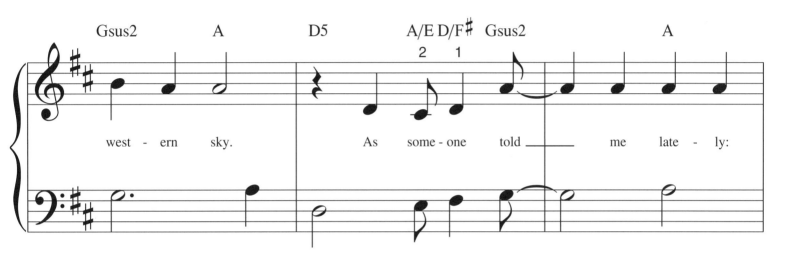

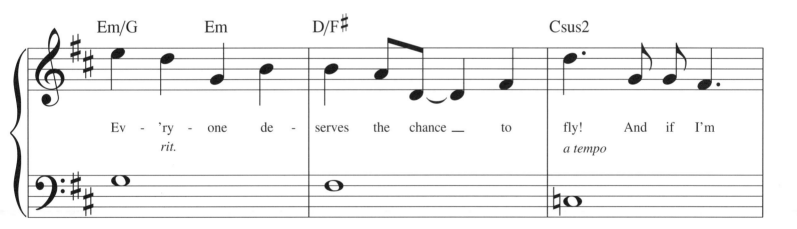

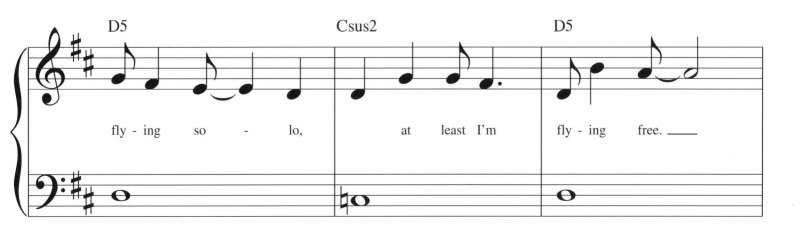

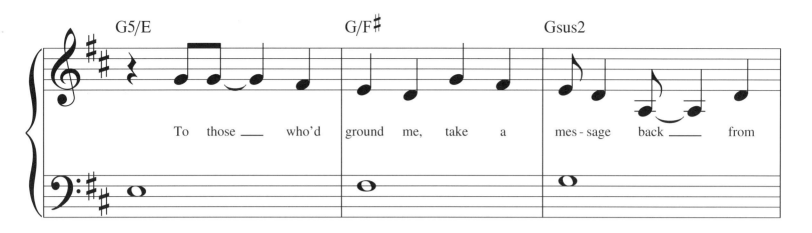

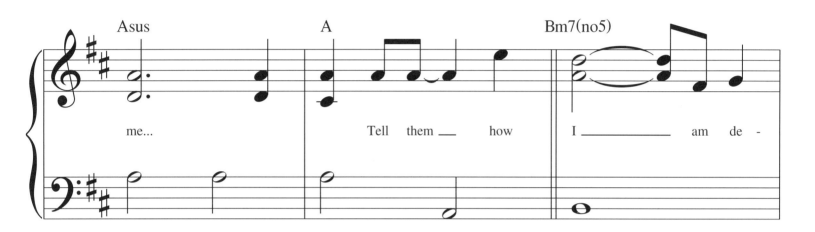

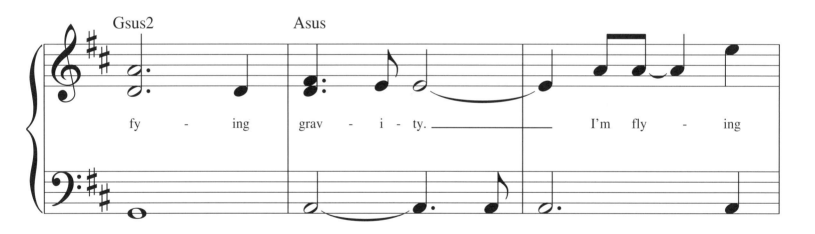

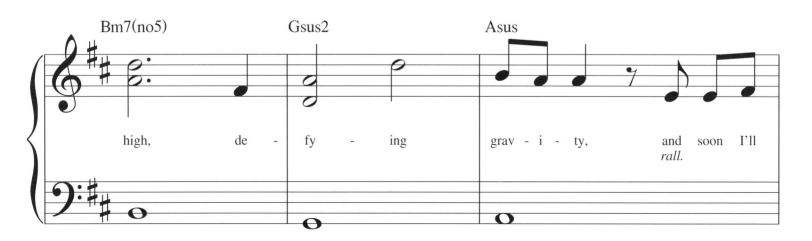

DING-DONG! THE WITCH IS DEAD

from THE WIZARD OF OZ

Lyric by E.Y. "YIP" HARBURG
Music by HAROLD ARLEN

EMBRACEABLE YOU

from CRAZY FOR YOU

Music and Lyrics by GEORGE GERSHWIN
and IRA GERSHWIN

Lyrics:

Em - brace me, my sweet em - brace - a - ble you! _
I love all the man - y charms a - bout you! _

Em - brace me, you ir - re -
A - bove all, I want my

place - a - ble you! _
arms a - bout you! _

Just one look at you, my heart grew

FORTY-SECOND STREET
from 42nd STREET

Words by AL DUBIN
Music by HARRY WARREN

it's the song I love the mel-o-dy of, _____

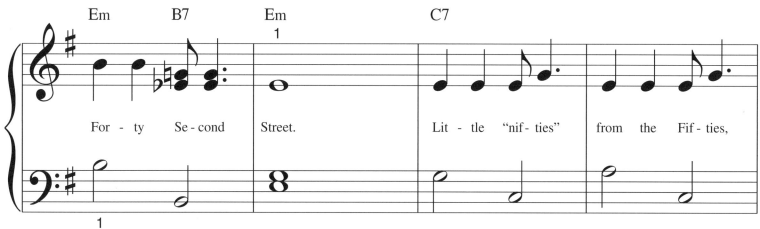

For-ty Se-cond Street. Lit-tle "nif-ties" from the Fif-ties,

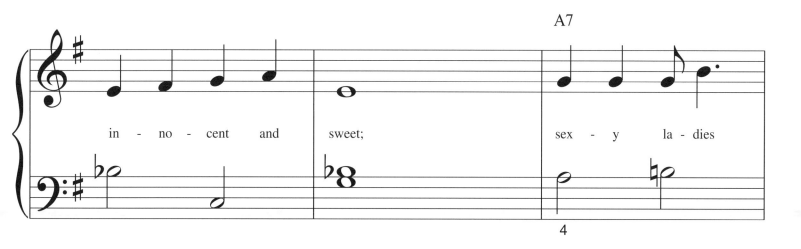

in - no - cent and sweet; sex - y la - dies

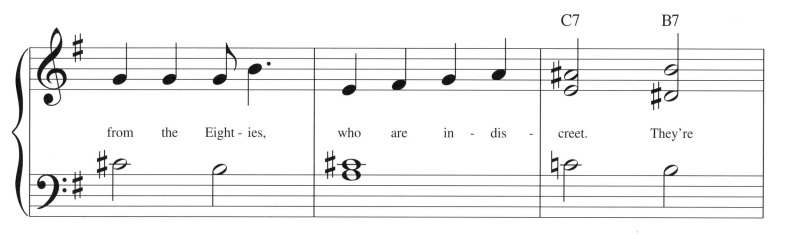

from the Eight-ies, who are in-dis-creet. They're

HERNANDO'S HIDEAWAY
from THE PAJAMA GAME

Words and Music by RICHARD ADLER
and JERRY ROSS

34

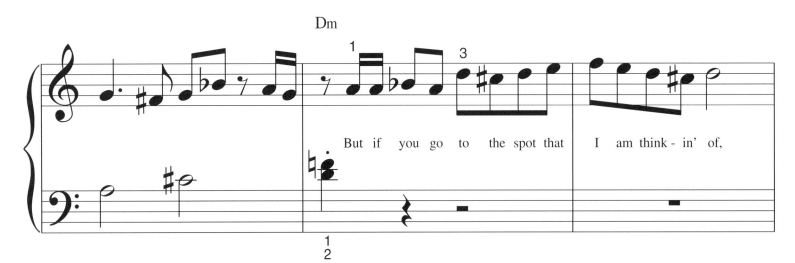

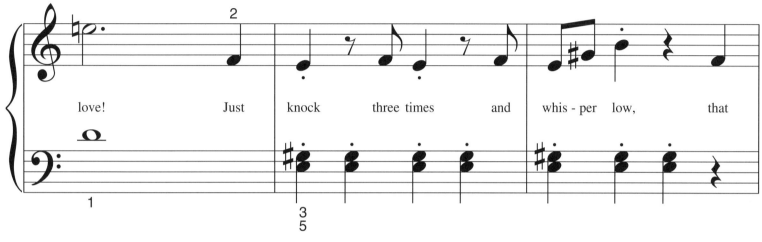

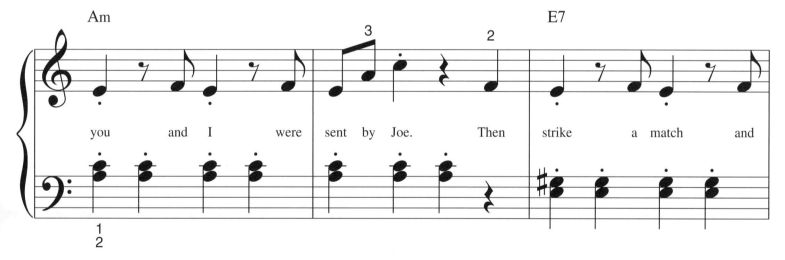

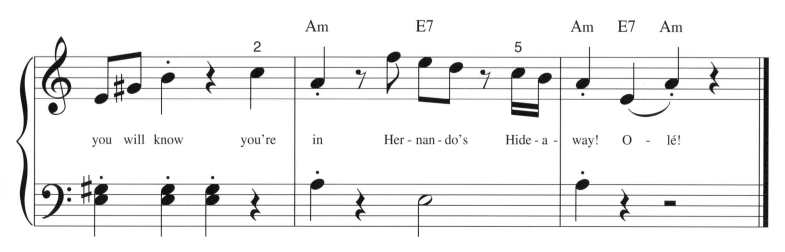

GOOD MORNING STARSHINE

from the Broadway Musical Production HAIR

Words by JAMES RADO and GEROME RAGNI
Music by GALT MacDERMONT

HEY THERE
from THE PAJAMA GAME

Words and Music by RICHARD ADLER
and JERRY ROSS

Hey there, you with the stars in your eyes, love nev-er made a fool of you, you used to be too wise! Hey there, you on that high fly-ing

HOW LONG HAS THIS BEEN GOING ON?

from ROSALIE

Music and Lyrics by GEORGE GERSHWIN
and IRA GERSHWIN

Moderately slow

I could cry salt - y tears;

where have I been all these years?

Lit - tle wow, ____
Lis - ten, you, ____

tell me now. How long has this been go - ing on?
tell me, do. How long has this been go - ing on?

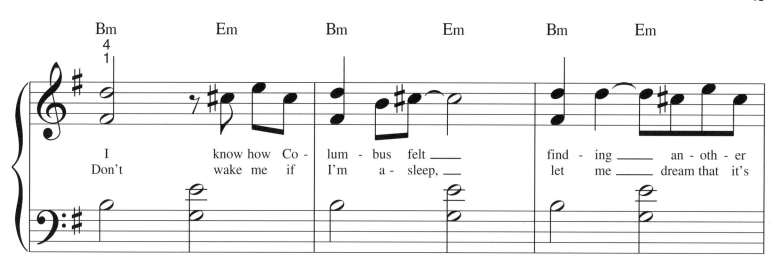

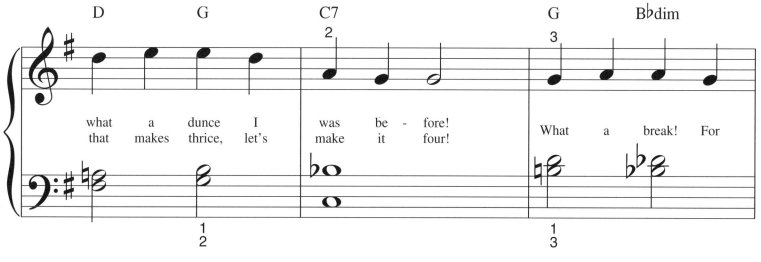

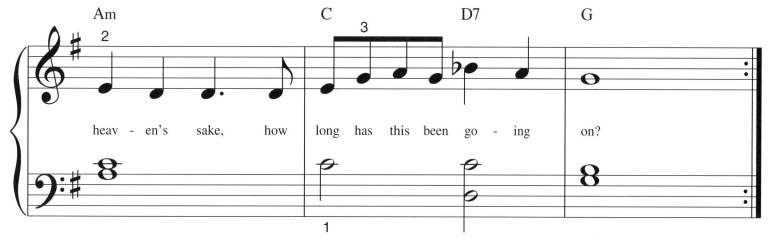

I ONLY HAVE EYES FOR YOU

from DAMES

Words by AL DUBIN
Music by HARRY WARREN

I GOT PLENTY O' NUTTIN'

from PORGY AND BESS®

Music and Lyrics by GEORGE GERSHWIN,
DuBOSE and DOROTHY HEYWARD
and IRA GERSHWIN

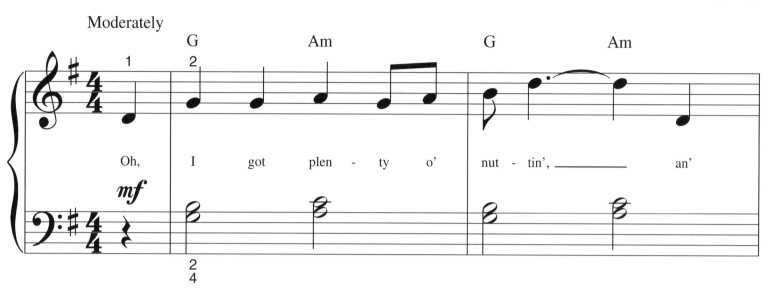

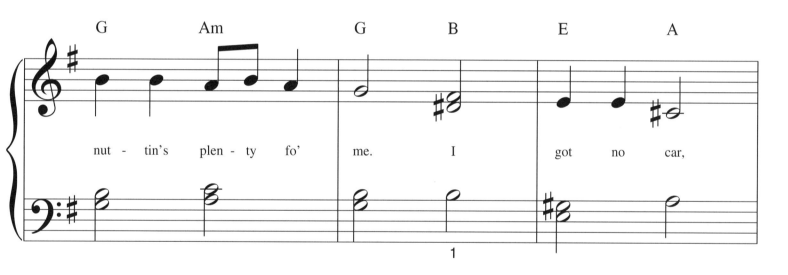

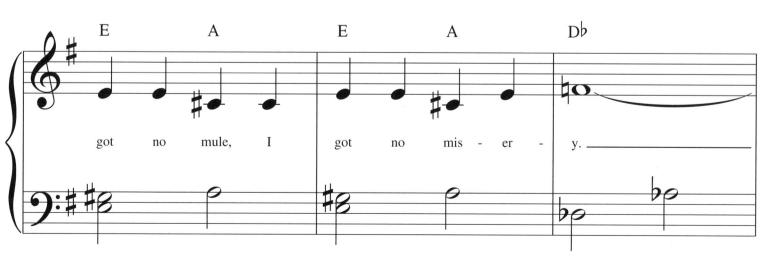

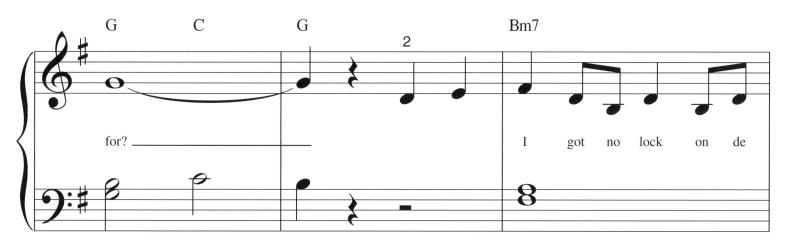

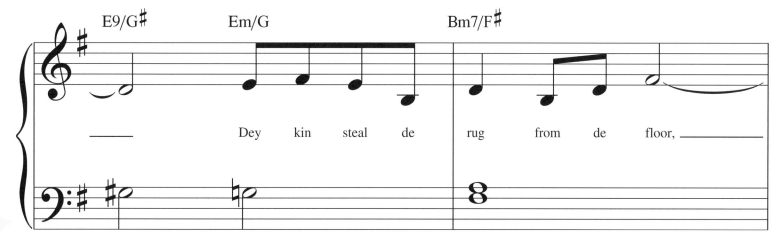

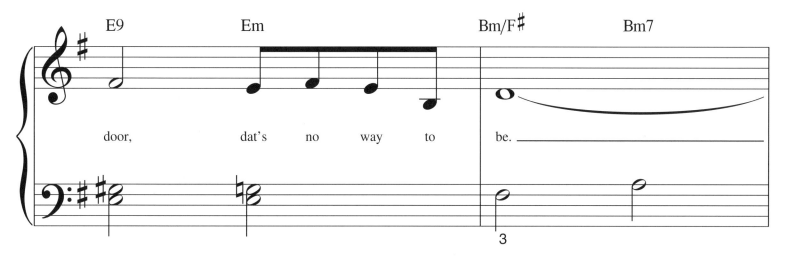

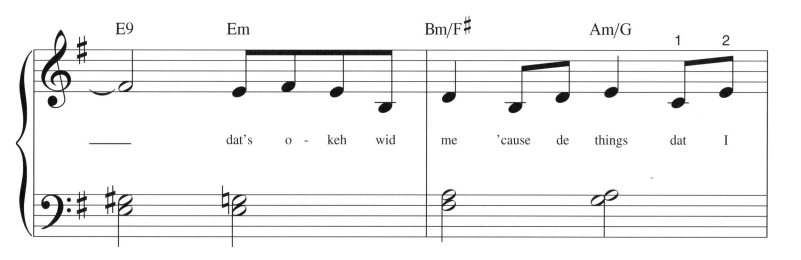

IF I ONLY HAD A BRAIN

from THE WIZARD OF OZ

Lyric by E.Y. "YIP" HARBURG
Music by HAROLD ARLEN

ISN'T IT A PITY?
from PARDON MY ENGLISH

Music and Lyrics by GEORGE GERSHWIN
and IRA GERSHWIN

It's a fun - ny thing: I look at you,

I get a thrill I nev - er knew. Is - n't it a pit - y

we nev - er met be - fore?

LITTLE JAZZ BIRD

from LADY, BE GOOD!

Music and Lyrics by GEORGE GERSHWIN
and IRA GERSHWIN

IT AIN'T NECESSARILY SO

from PORGY AND BESS ®

Music and Lyrics by GEORGE GERSHWIN,
DuBOSE and DOROTHY HEYWARD
and IRA GERSHWIN

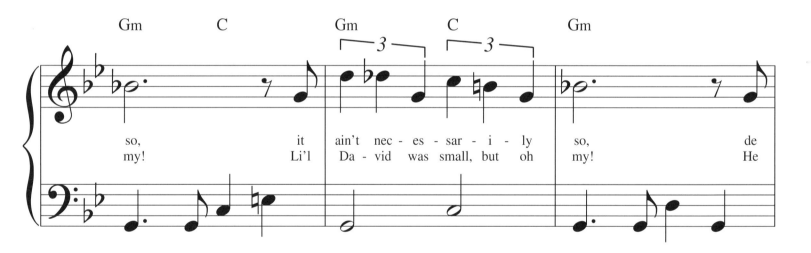

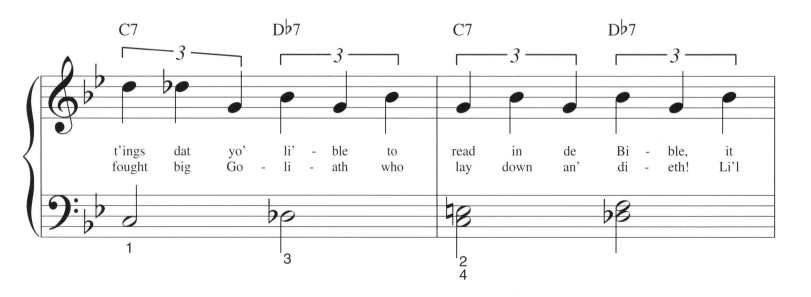

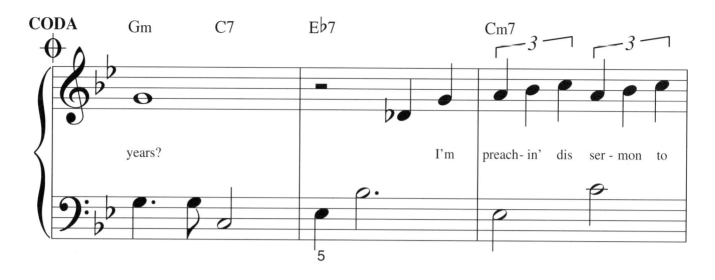

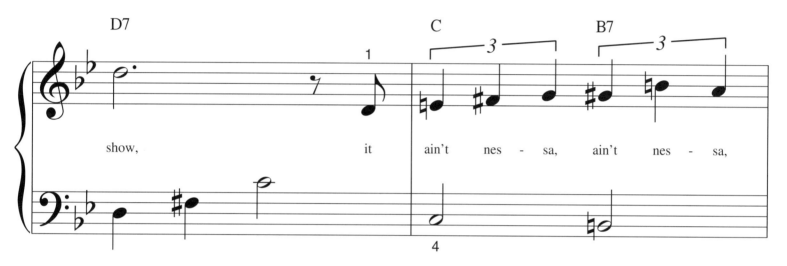

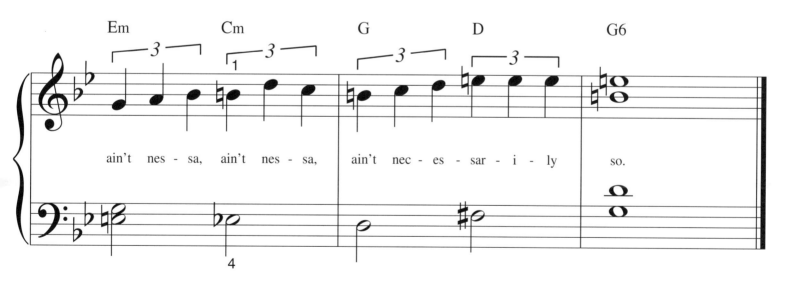

Additional Lyrics

3. Oh, Jonah, he lived in de whale,
   Oh, Jonah, he lived in de whale,
   Fo' he made his home in dat fish's abdomen.
   Oh, Jonah, he lived in de whale.

4. Li'l Moses was found in a stream,
   Li'l Moses was found in a stream,
   He floated on water till ol' Pharaoh's daughter,
   She fished him, she said, from that stream.

LULLABY OF BROADWAY
from 42nd STREET

Words by AL DUBIN
Music by HARRY WARREN

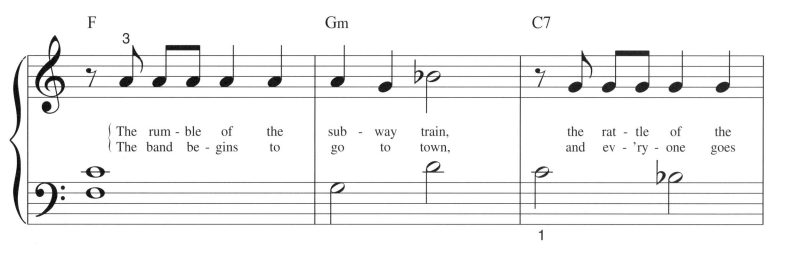

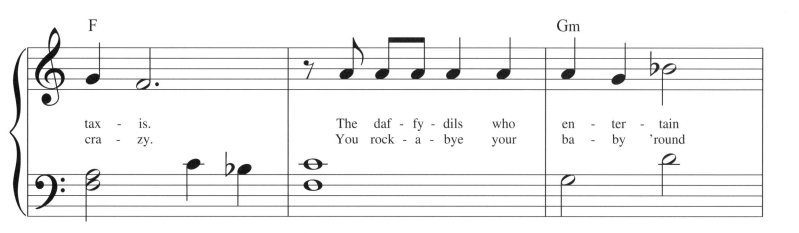

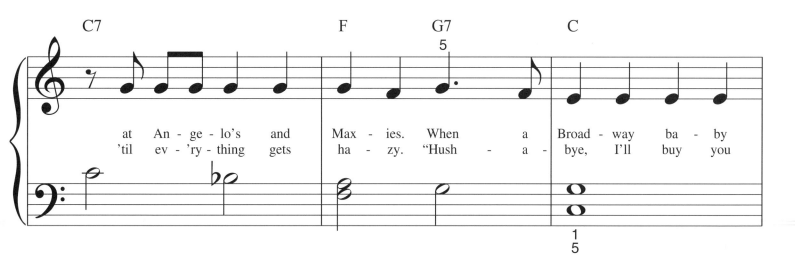

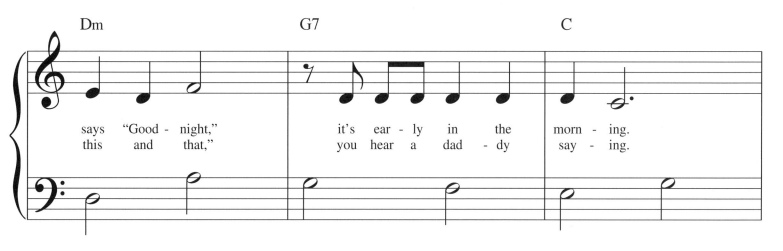

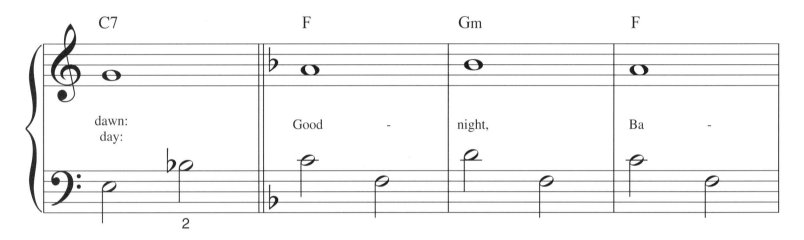

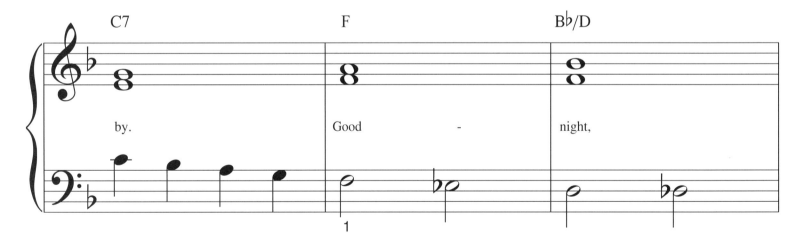

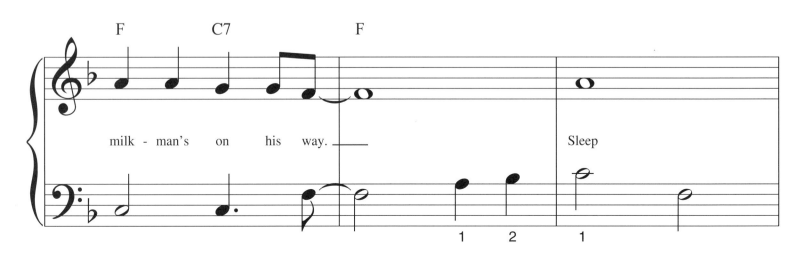

MACK THE KNIFE
from THE THREEPENNY OPERA

English Words by MARC BLITZSTEIN
Original German Words by BERT BRECHT
Music by KURT WEILL

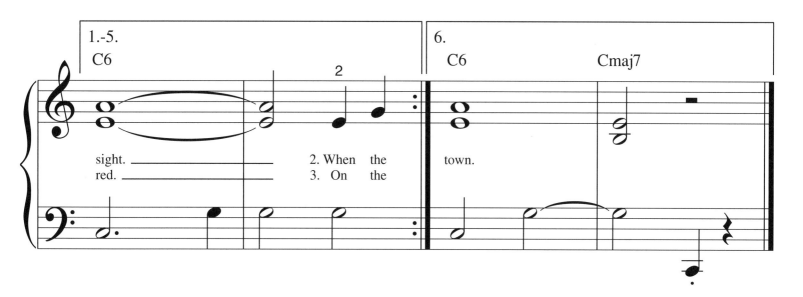

Additional Lyrics

3. On the sidewalk Sunday morning
   Lies a body oozing life.
   Someone's sneaking 'round the corner.
   Is the someone Mack the Knife?

4. From a tugboat by the river,
   a cement bag's dropping down.
   The cement's just for the weight, dear.
   Bet you Mackie's back in town.

5. Louie Miller disappeared, dear,
   After drawing out his cash.
   And Macheath spends like a sailor.
   Did our boy do something rash?

6. Sukey Tawdry, Jenny Diver,
   Polly Peachum, Lucy Brown.
   Oh, the line forms on the right, dear,
   Now that Mackie's back in town.

NEW YORK, NEW YORK

from ON THE TOWN

Lyrics by BETTY COMDEN and ADOLPH GREEN
Music by LEONARD BERNSTEIN

NICE WORK IF YOU CAN GET IT

from A DAMSEL IN DISTRESS

Music and Lyrics by GEORGE GERSHWIN
and IRA GERSHWIN

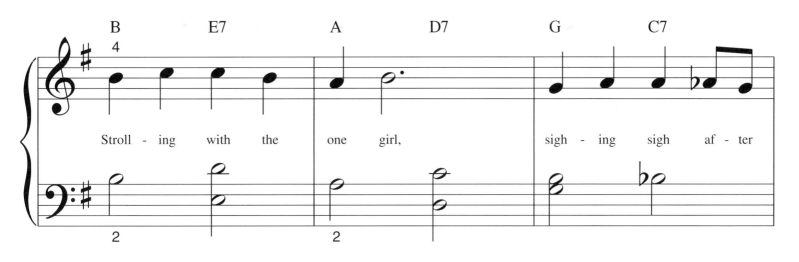

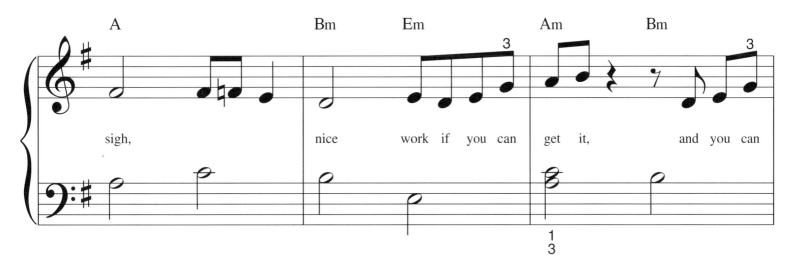

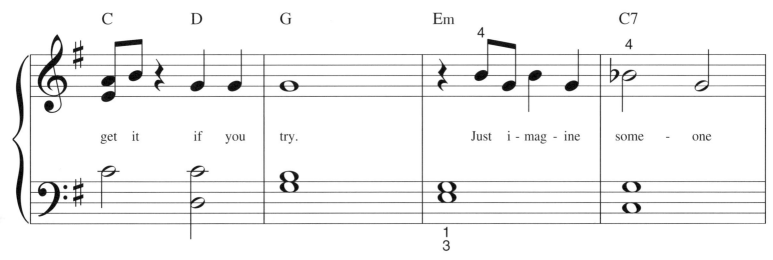

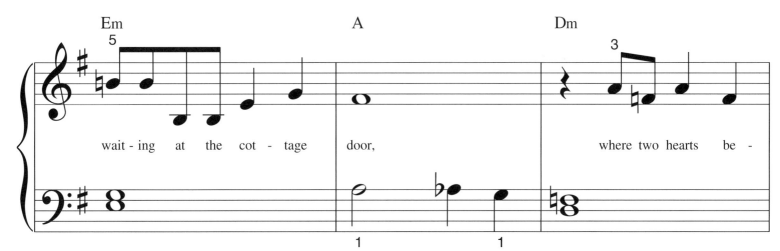

OVER THE RAINBOW
from THE WIZARD OF OZ

Music by HAROLD ARLEN
Lyric by E.Y. "YIP" HARBURG

Moderately, with freedom

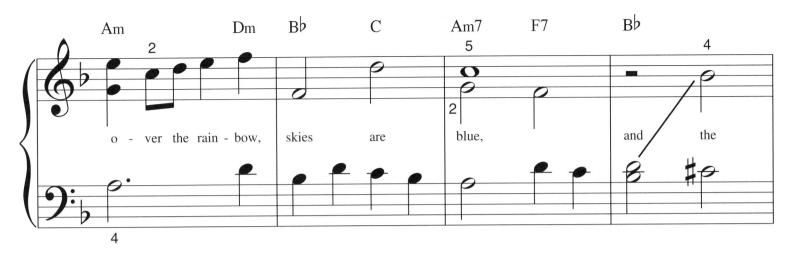

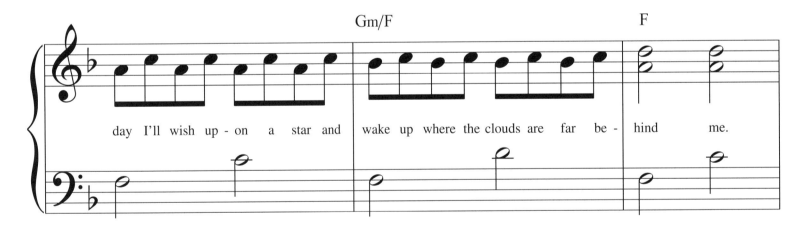

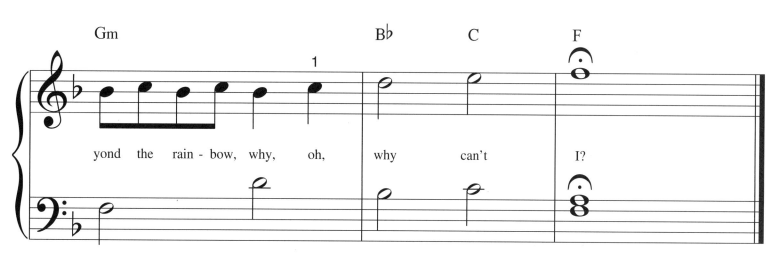

'S WONDERFUL
from FUNNY FACE

Music and Lyrics by GEORGE GERSHWIN
and IRA GERSHWIN

SEND IN THE CLOWNS
from A LITTLE NIGHT MUSIC

Words and Music by
STEPHEN SONDHEIM

SOMEONE TO WATCH OVER ME

from OH, KAY!

Music and Lyrics by GEORGE GERSHWIN
and IRA GERSHWIN

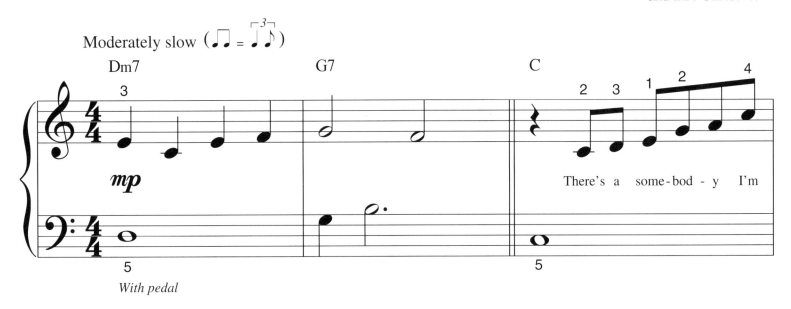

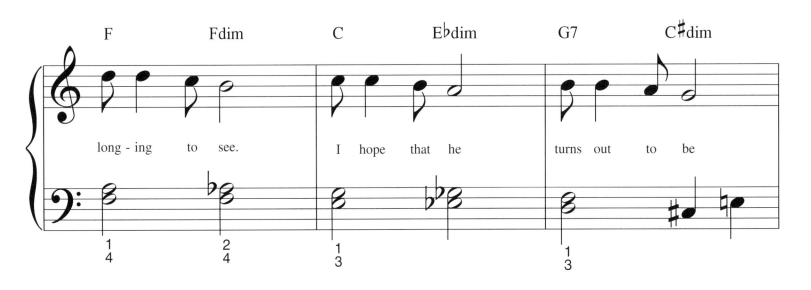

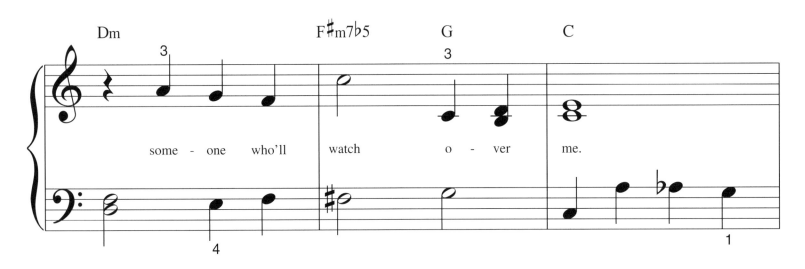

STRIKE UP THE BAND
from STRIKE UP THE BAND

Music and Lyrics by GEORGE GERSHWIN
and IRA GERSHWIN

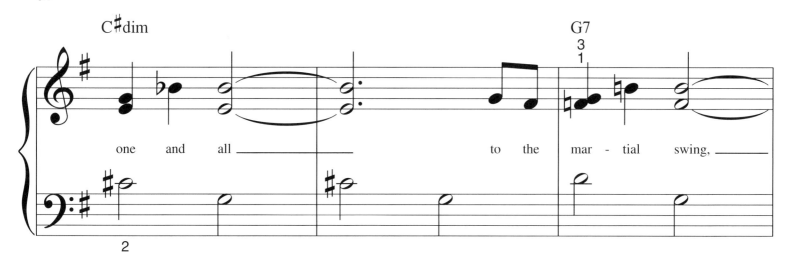

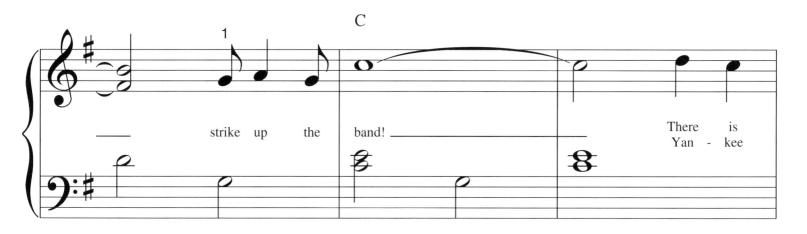

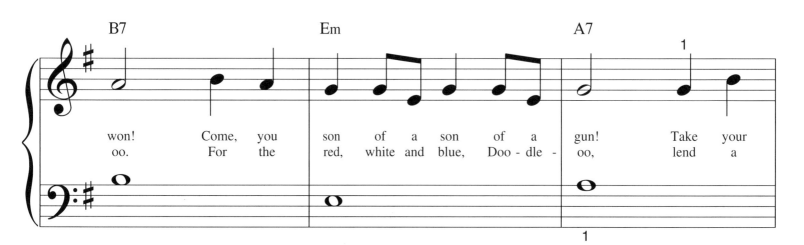

SUDDENLY
from LES MISÉRABLES

Music by CLAUDE-MICHEL SCHÖNBERG
Lyrics by HERBERT KRETZMER and ALAIN BOUBLIL

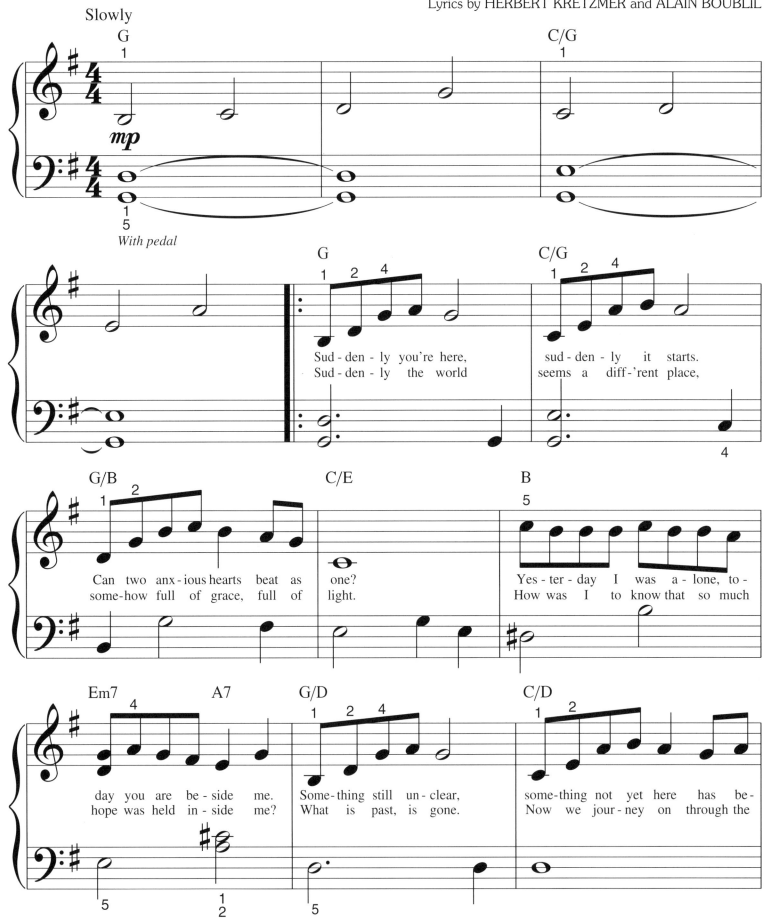

YOU'RE GETTING TO BE
A HABIT WITH ME

from 42nd STREET

Lyrics by AL DUBIN
Music by HARRY WARREN

THERE'S A BOAT DAT'S LEAVIN' SOON FOR NEW YORK

from *PORGY AND BESS*®

Music and Lyrics by GEORGE GERSHWIN,
IRA GERSHWIN, DuBOSE and DOROTHY HEYWARD

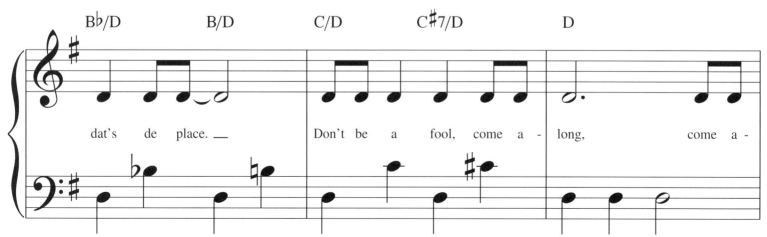

WE'RE OFF TO SEE THE WIZARD

from THE WIZARD OF OZ

Lyric by E.Y. "YIP" HARBURG
Music by HAROLD ARLEN

BIG FUN WITH BIG-NOTE PIANO BOOKS!
These songbooks feature exciting easy arrangements
for beginning piano students.

Elton John – Greatest Hits
16 of his biggest hits, including: Bennie and the Jets • Candle in the Wind • Crocodile Rock • Rocket Man • Sacrifice • Your Song • and more.
00221832 .... $10.95

Les Misérables
14 favorites from the Broadway sensation arranged for beginning pianists. Titles include: At the End of the Day • Bring Him Home • Castle on a Cloud • I Dreamed a Dream • In My Life • On My Own • Who Am I? • and more.
00221812 .... $14.95

Movie Hits
20 songs popularized on the silver screen, including: Breakaway • I Believe I Can Fly • I Will Remember You • Kokomo • Somewhere Out There • Tears in Heaven • What a Wonderful World • and more.
00221804 .... $10.95

The Phantom of the Opera
9 songs from the Broadway spectacular, including: All I Ask of You • Angel of Music • Masquerade • The Music of the Night • The Phantom of the Opera • The Point of No Return • Prima Donna • Think of Me • Wishing You Were Somehow Here Again.
00110006 .... $12.95

Pride & Prejudice
MUSIC FROM THE MOTION PICTURE SOUNDTRACK
12 piano pieces from the 2006 Oscar-nominated film: Another Dance • Darcy's Letter • Georgiana • Leaving Netherfield • Liz on Top of the World • Meryton Townhall • The Secret Life of Daydreams • Stars and Butterflies • and more.
00316125 .... $12.99

The Sound of Music
arranged by Phillip Keveren
9 favorites: Climb Ev'ry Mountain • Do-Re-Mi • Edelweiss • The Lonely Goatherd • Maria • My Favorite Things • Sixteen Going on Seventeen • So Long, Farewell • The Sound of Music.
00316057 .... $10.99

Today's Pop Hits
14 of today's hottest hits: Beautiful • Clocks • Complicated • Don't Know Why • Drift Away • Fallen • Heaven • A Moment Like This • 100 Years • Pieces of Me • She Will Be Loved • A Thousand Miles • You Don't Know My Name • You Raise Me Up.
00221817 .... $12.95

Worship Favorites
20 powerful songs: Above All • Come, Now Is the Time to Worship • I Could Sing of Your Love Forever • More Precious Than Silver • Open the Eyes of My Heart • Shout to the Lord • and more.
00311207 .... $10.95

Best of Adele
Now even beginners can play their favorite Adele tunes! This book features big-note arrangements of 10 top songs: Chasing Pavements • Daydreamer • Hometown Glory • Lovesong • Make You Feel My Love • One and Only • Rolling in the Deep • Set Fire to the Rain • Someone like You • Turning Tables.
00308601 .... $12.99

Beatles' Best
27 classics for beginners to enjoy, including: Can't Buy Me Love • Eleanor Rigby • Hey Jude • Michelle • Here, There and Everywhere • When I'm Sixty-Four • Yesterday • and more.
00222561 .... $14.99

The Best Songs Ever
70 favorites, featuring: Body and Soul • Crazy • Edelweiss • Fly Me to the Moon • Georgia on My Mind • Imagine • The Lady Is a Tramp • Memory • A String of Pearls • Tears in Heaven • Unforgettable • You Are So Beautiful • and more.
00310425 .... $19.95

Children's Favorite Movie Songs
arranged by Phillip Keveren
16 favorites from films, including: The Bare Necessities • Beauty and the Beast • Can You Feel the Love Tonight • Do-Re-Mi • The Rainbow Connection • Tomorrow • Zip-A-Dee-Doo-Dah • and more.
00310838 .... $10.95

Classical Music's Greatest Hits
24 beloved classical pieces, including: Air on the G String • Ave Maria • By the Beautiful Blue Danube • Canon in D • Eine Kleine Nachtmusik • Für Elise • Ode to Joy • Romeo and Juliet • Waltz of the Flowers • more.
00310475 .... $9.95

Country Hits for Big-Note Piano
14 country classics: Amazed • Bless the Broken Road • Blue • Breathe • Concrete Angel • I Hope You Dance • Jesus Take the Wheel • You're Still the One • and more.
00311815 .... $10.95

Disney Big-Note Collection
Over 40 Disney favorites, including: Circle of Life • Colors of the Wind • Hakuna Matata • It's a Small World • Under the Sea • A Whole New World • Winnie the Pooh • Zip-A-Dee-Doo-Dah • and more.
00316056 .... $19.99

Essential Classical
22 simplified piano pieces from top composers, including: Ave Maria (Schubert) • Blue Danube Waltz (Strauss) • Für Elise (Beethoven) • Jesu, Joy of Man's Desiring (Bach) • Morning (Grieg) • Pomp and Circumstance (Elgar) • and many more.
00311205 .... $9.95

Favorite Children's Songs
arranged by Bill Boyd
29 easy arrangements of songs to play and sing with children: Peter Cottontail • I Whistle a Happy Tune • It's a Small World • On the Good Ship Lollipop • The Rainbow Connection • and more!
00240251 .... $10.95